HOW I SURVIVED THE WILDERNESS OF LIFE AND EMERGE A HAPPY PERSON DESPITE LIFE'S CHALLENGES/PROBLEMS

A-Z PRACTICAL STEPS TOWARDS HAPPINESS & SELF MOTIVATION

RYAN SMITH

Copyright © 2018 Ryan Smith

All rights reserved.

ISBN: 9781726651547

DEDICATION

This work is dedicated to the Most Holy Trinity, the source of true happiness, through the hands of the Blessed Virgin Mary.

CONTENTS

	Acknowledgments	i
1	INTRODUCTION	3
2	WHAT IS HAPPINESS?	4
3	A-Z PRACTICAL STEPS TOWARDS HAPPINESS	10
4	CONCLUSION	28

ACKNOWLEDGMENTS

This to acknowledge the sorrows and worries encountered by various people in the world. I want you all to know that there could be tears at night but joy comes with dawn. Your sorrows will not last forever but pass away soon as I urge you all to rise above your situations and focus on the
bright side of life since there is always a silver lining behind every dark cloud.

1 INTRODUCTION

It is no gainsay that "life is not a bird of roses." This saying is an attestation to the fact that it is not every time that things will go our way. Things are bound to go wrong sometimes no matter how proactive or predictive we are. There will always be moments of ups and downs, success and failure. Adversities are bound to come our way no matter the efforts we make to avert them. Do not feel that I am sounding sadistic but it is just the bitter truth/reality of life. However, this reality does not mean we shouldn't make efforts to achieve great feat and enjoy life to the fullest and avert difficulties. The fact however remains that a disposition towards any eventuality of life be it positive or negative event will do us more good than harm. This will go a long way to make us undaunted and emerge victorious amidst the joys, difficulties, toils and disappointments of life.

2 WHAT IS HAPPINESS?

Happiness does not connote lack of problems, challenges, disasters or misfortunes. It is rather a state of mind that enables an individual to maintain a positive disposition towards life events or occurrences. This definition contains some key words that need further explanation and these include: *mind, positive disposition, events or occurrences and individual.*

The Mind: this refers to the conscious rationalization capacity of humans and it is this capacity that separates human beings from lower animals. As such, this capacity makes them beings that cannot be pushed, by life difficulties or life events, from one extreme to the other like pre-determined pendulum bulbs.

> 1. STIMULUS (LIFE EVENTS)--------→ UNINFORMED REACTIONS (SORROW, HAPPINESS)

The illustration above shows a situation where individuals unconsciously react or respond to situations without being consciously aware of their reactions. On the other hand, the illustration below shows a situation where individuals consciously rationalize life events before reacting or responding to them.

> 2. STIMULUS (LIFE EVENTS) → RATIONALIZATION → INFORMED REACTIONS (SORROW, HAPPINESS)

Therefore, the capacity to rationalize does not just make humans conscious of happenings around them but also enables them to consciously rationalize events or life difficulties and find solutions to them. There are two aspects of the mind: rational and irrational thinking patterns.

Disposition: this refers to one's tendency to respond either positively or negatively to life events or occurrences. There are two types of disposition, namely: positive and negative dispositions. These dispositions are informed by our thinking patterns which could either be rational or irrational thinking patterns. These thinking patterns are rooted in our beliefs about life. It is these thinking patterns that determine our dispositions towards life events.

> RATIONAL THINKING PATTERN = POSITIVE DISPOSITIONS TOWARDS LIFE EVENTS. IRRATIONAL THINKING PATTERN = NEGATIVE DISPOSITIONS TOWARDS LIFE EVENTS.

Events: Life could be compared to a bird with two wings or a coin that is two sided. Once one of the wings is removed then the bird will no longer be able to fly, nor will a coin remain a coin if a side of it is removed. In the same vein, life is full of ups and downs, fortunes and misfortunes, successes and failures, ill health and good health, accidents and safety, poverty and riches, deaths and aliveness, etc. Experience has shown that we all have our share in the fortunes and misfortunes of life. This shows that life's events or situations cannot always go our way. As such, a person that is alive today and wish to always be alive may be dead tomorrow, a wealthy person today may become poor tomorrow, a winner/champion will not always be on top no matter how good he or she is, a person who is cancer stricken today may be freed from it tomorrow, a successful person of today may encounter failure tomorrow. "Is there any human being that is totally free from and unconcerned with these realities of life?" "I doubt, but if there is then such person will be a lifeless corpse that lacks awareness about life, that is not touched in any way by life occurrences". This is the paradox we find ourselves in and it goes a long way to shape us and make us strong depending on our dispositions towards them. The question is: "can we still live happily despite these paradoxes, despite the misfortunes of life." The answer is "YES". How this happiness can be achieved will be explicated as you read on.

Individuals: no two human beings, not even identical twins are exactly the same in everything. There is always something that distinguishes one person from the other and this makes us unique individuals. In the same vein our life experiences/events/encounters are not exactly the same nor do we view or respond to them in exactly the same way. There is always something unique in the way we respond to life events. Hence, it will be sheer absurdity to compare yourself to another person and wish to live exactly the way the other person does. Even if things are seemingly going fine for the other person, it is still improper to desire to be in the shoe of the other person because you don't know where the shoe pinches him, he alone knows. This does not mean that we cannot learn from others or improve our lives as a result of what we learn from others, but to be lost in the admiration of the lives of others or to want to emulate them blindly is a disservice to one's self.

3 A-Z PRACTICAL STEPS TOWARDS HAPPINESS

ACKNOWLEDGE AND ACCEPT

Acknowledge and accept life for what it is. The world is a place we live in and we will depart it after some time. Therefore, accept and manage what you cannot change and improve on what you can change. Know yourself for who you are and accept your personality while making great efforts to improve on yourself. Also acknowledge and accept others for their identity. You may offer wise advice (never impose this) to people but accept their final decisions for what it is regardless of your understanding of their beliefs, motives or activities.

BUILD

Build for yourself a genuine family and friends you can share your genuine concerns with. A family that can freely and willingly share in your dreams, pains, worries, happiness and achievements without the feeling of animosity or negative jealousy.

CONSCIENCE

Cultivate and develop your conscience. Never ever allow it to be killed by your misdeeds or the so many atrocities going on around you for a person whose conscience is dead is a living corpse waiting to be buried and a condemned criminal that is hopeless. It is your secret judge. Examine it on daily basis before sleeping off and it is a voice must be obeyed if you don't want to live a life that is full of regrets.

DETERMINATION

Determine to be fruitful and achieving in your worthwhile and good endeavours, while making and persevering in the right efforts no matter the sacrifice it takes. The roadblocks and obstacles along the way will finally serve as stepping stones. Success will surely be yours with such attitude.

EXPLORATION

Explore and tryout new frontiers of opportunities for the world has so much to offer, while you also have so much to give. Always be open-minded and every time you take a stab at something new, you will discover new things about yourself.

F

FORGIVENESS

It may sometimes be very difficult to forgive depending on the magnitude of the offence. It takes a great sacrifice and resolutions to let go of grudges but remember the benefits of forgiveness far outweigh our grudges because it is a royal road to happiness and peace of mind. Always make fresh and determined efforts and resolutions to forgive each time you remember what the person has done to you. However, forgiveness does not necessarily mean that you must return to the same mode of relationship or dealings with the person that has offended you if such relationship is hurting but you must at least forgive so as to be able to maintain your own peace of mind and move on. You can't move on without this peace of mind.

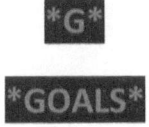

GOALS

We all have various aspirations and goals in life. Examine your goals and make sure they are genuine and not an intrusion to the life of your fellows. However, separate yourself or break away from everything that obstructs your efforts to achieve your genuine dreams and aspirations and make the right efforts to achieve these no matter the sacrifices (these should be just/moral anyway) you have to pay. But remember, *nothing says things must go your way no matter how great your efforts are. So do not be discouraged if your efforts do not yield at any point of the journey of life. Rather, accept such disappointments as part of life and try to make new efforts and persevere having learnt from your mistakes.*

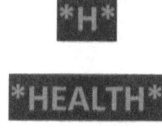

HEALTH

Health is wealth and as such deserves to be preserved with utmost care. Always eat well and eat right. Exercise and relax your mind appropriately (worry less) if you want to have good health of mind and body without becoming the doctor's money making tool. However, do not delay in seeing your doctor if need be.

IGNORE

Overlook the negative voice that discourages you and makes you feel you can't achieve. Focus rather on your goals and let your previous achievements remind you of your greatness and the possibilities of achieving greater feats with the right effort.

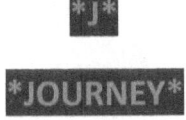

JOURNEY

Life is like a script and a journey through the wilderness (no one can say what the future holds for sure). It is full of so many ups and downs. However, remember that happiness is your right and choice in this journey no matter how difficult things may seem.

KNOW

Know that there is always something positive about whatever befalls us regardless of how terrible things may appear, just that we most times get emotionally blindfolded. If only we can think independently of our emotions and rise above our problems/challenges, then we will be able to manage most of the misfortunes that come our way and some of them will hardly shake us. Remember, "There is always a silver lining behind every dark cloud".

LOVE

Love is a sacred road to endless happiness. However, individuals must first learn to love no matter who we are displaying our love to without expecting anything in return. If we live this way, love will surely follow us and happiness will be ours forever.

Never overlook the poor, the sick, the defenseless, the powerless and those suffering from one affliction or the other regardless of your relationship with them. Give them a helping hand and be generous to them whenever you can and make them realize the potentials and hopes that lie within them.

Have you seen a situation whereby you just

feel happy despite being hated by your fellows? Yes, it is possible because you have given them unconditional love to the best of your ability. Be happy to give rather than receive love.

M
MANAGE

Manage your time and expenses wisely, minding the fact that time is precious and the present day economy is harsh. Spend your time on what is profitable because a wasted time can never be regained. Learn to manage your income and never ever live above it, otherwise your worries will be compounded and you will soon break down. Don't buy/do things because friends/others are buying/doing them because your pockets and nature are not the same.

N

* NONENTITY *

Never ever look down on yourself or others in life. That things seem not going the way you want them does not mean that you are useless. We are all endowed with boundless potentials that we need to develop in order to unleash the greatness in us. Therefore, look deep into yourself and discover what you are good at or what you seem to be good at and develop it to the best of your ability.

O

OPEN

Open your mind and eyes and see the magnificence/beauty of created things (sky, deep blue sea, flowers, humans, etc) around you. Contemplate and admire them for they point to their creator. This practice can elicit good feelings in you and bring you closer to your Maker whose Almighty hand can turn the worst situation around.

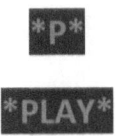

"All work and no play makes Jack a dull boy." Therefore, always find time to catch fun no matter your busy schedule. Fun has a way of making us physically and mentally sound.

Do not hesitate to ask questions when you need to especially when you are confused. It goes a long way to keep our memories and minds updated but remember the wilderness of life contains certain mysteries that your mind will not be able to unravel. Accept these mysteries and enjoy life to the best of your ability.

RELATIONSHIP/FRIENDSHIP

It is no gainsay that "no man is an island." We all need each other to make life worthwhile. Even the rich need the poor to share their wealth with if life must make meaning to them, for what is the benefit of acquired wealth that cannot benefit others? Therefore we need to make great efforts to build a solid relationship with families and friends. True friendship is hard to come by but if you have a reliable friend then cherish the person the way you cherish yourself for a friend is oneself in another body. If you want to make friendship/relationship worthwhile, then you and your friends must possess the following qualities and friends of this nature must be kept forever because they will be the shoulder you can lean on when the going gets tough. The following friends must be cherished and kept:

Those who are honest to you. These people open up their hearts and tell you the truth about yourself and about themselves even if it hurts.

Those who empathize with you and come to your aid during your difficult moments as well as genuinely share your success with you.

Those who despite their care for you appreciate the fact that you are a unique individual, and as such, respect your decisions and privacy.

Those who despite your weaknesses still go ahead to see your potentials, encourage you and inspire you to be the best you can be.

Those who have proven to be dependable and reliable over time.

Those who freely and willingly give to you not minding whether you give to them or not.

SELF-GIVING

Life is neither all about money nor personal gains. There is need to sometimes share your abilities, knowledge, talents, aptitudes, time, energy with the intention of improving the lives of others without expecting anything in return. This will surely return to you in manifest fold in ways you cannot imagine.

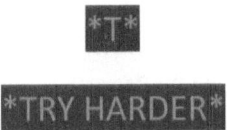

TRY HARDER

Always remain dedicated to your works and endeavours and enjoy doing them as you make every good effort to achieve your dreams even when this seems impossible or difficult. But always remember that anything can happen in life. So be happy when your hopes come true and never kill yourself or worry so much like the hopeless when things go wrong (about your failures). However, learn from your mistakes, try harder and move on.

UTILIZE

Utilize your endowments to your best capacity. A squandered talent or aptitude is profitless and has no esteem. However, talents/abilities made into endeavors will bring surprising prizes.

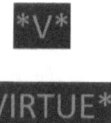

VIRTUE

Virtue enhances our personalities and character. The great personalities of this world (Martin Luther King Jr., Mahatma Gandhi, Nelson Mandela, mother Theresa of Calcuta, St. Pio of Pietrelchina, St. John Paul II) are people of great virtues. Therefore, we must cultivate virtues and examine our progress in whatever virtue we choose to cultivate. It however requires great conscious efforts and sacrifices which are worth it at the end.

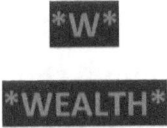

WEALTH

Wealth is surely not limited to money. We could be wealthy in various things. Whatever is the nature of your wealth, make sure you don't get engrossed in it. Do not allow your wealth to blindfold or tie you down or use you. Your engrossment in your wealth will surely bring you endless sorrows if anything goes wrong with it. Meanwhile, nothing guarantees that something will not go wrong with our wealth someday because the wealth in itself is fleeting. More so, do not use it to intimidate others. Rather, see it as something to be used not only to your benefits but also to the benefits of others. In this way, our wealth will bring us and those around us endless happiness.

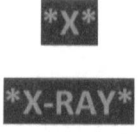

X-RAY

Do not be too quick to judge people's behavior or condemn them but dig deep into the rationale behind their actions. You may discover that things are not the way you think and so be able to excuse them. Even if you find them guilty, do no condemn them, rather give a helping hand because no one is perfect, not even you.

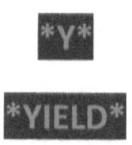

YIELD

Always yield to positive advice from those who are more experienced about life and those who seem to be vaster but remember even a child or that person you accord little or no respect can offer you a liberating advice. No one knows it all.

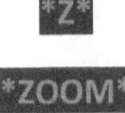

Zoom away from bad company/friends for bad company corrupts good morals. But you must first make great efforts to be good yourself, otherwise you will only keep attracting bad company.

4 CONCLUSION

Remember "happiness is your right and choice." Let nothing take this away from you. Things will surely go wrong at one point or the other but behind every dark cloud there is always a silver lining. Therefore, make great efforts even in your down times to discover the good side of things. This will surely help you to weather the storm of life. Grieve/cry when you need to because tears in itself brings about great psychological relief but don't grieve hopelessly and avoid grieving alone. Make efforts to share your problems with friends who really care. Letting out your problems to reliable and dependable friends bring about psychological relief.

ABOUT THE AUTHOR

I am a counseling psychologist, a life coach and a philosopher who is well experienced in happiness related matters.

www.ingramcontent.com/pod-product-compliance
Lightning Source LLC
Chambersburg PA
CBHW031559210526
45464CB00003B/1343